waffles & pancakes

Kate Habershon

waffles & pancakes

photography by William Lingwood

RYLAND
PETERS
& SMALL
LONDON NEW YORK

Designer Catherine Randy
Commissioning Editor Elsa Petersen-Schepelern
Production Patricia Harrington
Art Director Gabriella Le Grazie
Publishing Director Alison Starling

Food Stylist Kate Habershon
Cooking Assistant Becca Hetherston
Stylist Antonia Gaunt
Photographer's Assistant Emma Bentham-Wood

First published in Great Britain in 2002
by Ryland Peters & Small
Kirkman House, 12–14 Whitfield Street,
London W1T 2RP
www.rylandpeters.com

10 9 8 7 6 5 4 3 2 1

Text © Kate Habershon 2002
Design and photographs
© Ryland Peters & Small 2002

ISBN 1 84172 342 8

A catalogue record for this book is available from the
British Library.

Printed in China.

Notes

All spoon measurements are level
unless otherwise indicated. Batters
for pancakes and waffles vary in
consistency, which in turn affects
the accuracy of tablespoon
measurements. In this book,
tablespoon measures for mixed
batters should be taken as heaped,
rather than level.

The number of pancakes cooked in
each batch will depend on the size
of the frying pan used.

Waffle irons and waffle makers vary
in size. Most take about 125 ml of
batter. Spoon in just enough
mixture so that it almost covers the
base, leaving enough room for the
waffle to spread. Alternatively,
follow the manufacturer's instructions.

All eggs are medium, unless
otherwise specified. Uncooked or
partly cooked eggs should not be
served to the very young, the very
old, the frail, or to pregnant women.

contents

For a beautiful breakfast ...

The all-American breakfast, what image does that conjure? For me, it's pancakes and waffles piled high and loaded with butter, warm maple syrup and slices of crisp bacon. They appear on just about every breakfast menu, and as is typical in the United States, the choices are endless and often highly creative. Even the most modest diners offer their own unique variations, blueberry, ginger, pumpkin and potato. As for the toppings they are too numerous to list.

The word 'waffle' is derived from the old French word for 'honeycomb' and referred to the distinctive pattern made by the waffle iron. The style varies from region to region, from light and crisp, to heavy and buttery. But it is the Belgian version which is probably the most popular these days: with its crisp crust and silky interior, it is waffle perfection, and has found its way to all corners of the world.

In Europe, waffles and pancakes are associated less with home cooking and more with street food; a hot treat on a cold day out. It's common to find street vendors selling hot, sugar-dredged waffles, smothered in jam and cream. If you follow your nose, you'll find the nearest crêperie – the heavenly aroma of melted chocolate and spiced apples is hard to ignore.

While still strongly associated with breakfast, clearly waffles and pancakes are no longer confined to the breakfast table. With such a wide choice of toppings and consistencies, these simple batters can form the basis of a delicious meal or a delicious snack at any time of the day – enjoy! I have had enormous fun putting this book together – I do hope you have as much fun adding these recipes to your repertoire.

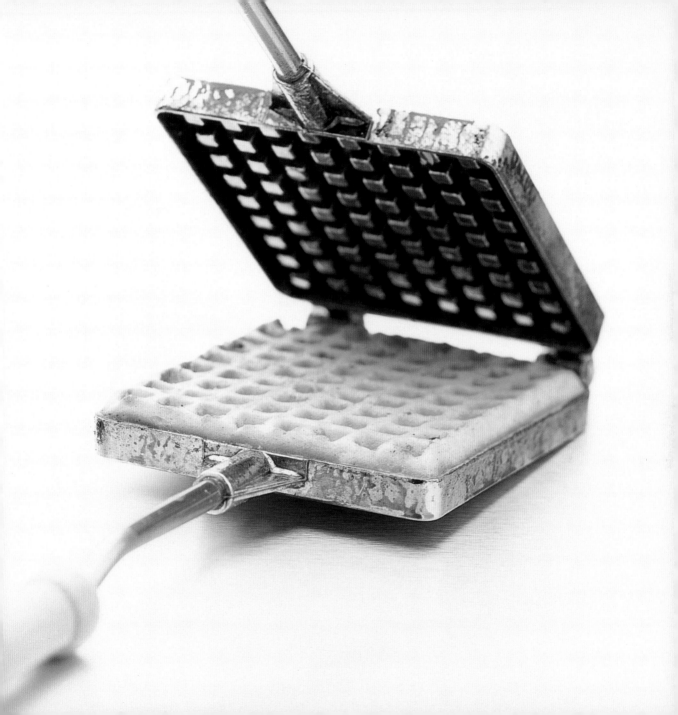

perfect pancakes

Everyone has a favourite pancake recipe and this is mine – well risen with a soft texture ready to soak up syrup like a sponge. Serve with your choice of fruit, syrups, cream or butter.

Simple Pancake Stack

285 g plain flour

2½ teaspoons baking powder

1 teaspoon salt

3 tablespoons caster sugar

225 ml milk

3 eggs

55 g unsalted butter, melted and cooled

To serve (optional)

maple syrup or other sauces (pages 60–63)

unsalted butter or whipped butter (page 16)

a flat griddle pan or frying pan, preheated and lightly greased

Serves 4

Makes 8 medium or 4 large pancakes

Sift the flour, baking powder, salt and sugar into a bowl. Put the milk, eggs and cooled melted butter into a second large bowl, then mix with a wire whisk. Add the sifted dry ingredients and whisk gently to make a thick batter. Be careful not to overwork the mixture – it doesn't matter if the batter isn't smooth.

Heat the prepared griddle or frying pan over medium heat. Reduce the heat. Pour about 3 tablespoons of batter into the pan and cook in batches of 3–4 for 1 minute over low heat until small bubbles begin to appear on the surface and the underside is golden brown. Turn the pancake over and cook the other side for 1 minute. Transfer to a plate and keep warm in a low oven while you cook the remainder – use 3 tablespoons of batter for each pancake.

Serve immediately with maple syrup and butter.

The all-American classic, loved by millions. Use fresh or frozen berries, but I prefer frozen because they take slightly longer to cook and don't burn so quickly.

Blueberry Sour Cream Pancakes
with Maple Syrup Pecans

285 g plain flour

2 teaspoons baking powder

1 teaspoon salt

55 g caster sugar

2 eggs, separated

250 ml sour cream

150 ml milk

55 g unsalted butter, melted
and cooled

250 g blueberries, fresh or frozen

vanilla ice cream, to serve

Maple syrup pecans

100 g pecan halves

250 ml maple syrup

55 g unsalted butter

a baking sheet

*a flat griddle pan or frying pan,
preheated and lightly greased*

Serves 4
Makes 8–10 pancakes

To make the maple syrup pecans, spread the nuts over a baking sheet and cook in a preheated oven at 200°C (400°F) Gas 6 for 5 minutes until lightly toasted. Simmer the maple syrup in a small saucepan for 3 minutes. Remove from the heat and stir in the pecans and butter.

To make the pancakes, sift the flour, baking powder, salt and sugar into a bowl. Put the egg yolks, sour cream, milk and butter into a second bowl and beat well, then add the flour mixture all at once and beat until smooth. Put the egg whites into a clean bowl and whisk until soft peaks form. Fold them gently into the batter, then fold in the blueberries. Do not to overmix – a few lumps of flour and egg white don't matter.

Heat the prepared griddle over medium heat. Reduce the heat. Pour 3 tablespoons of batter into the pan and cook in batches of 3–4 for 1–2 minutes over very low heat to avoid burning the blueberries, until small bubbles begin to appear on top and the underside is golden brown. Turn them over and cook the other side for 1 minute. Transfer to a plate and keep them warm in a low oven while you cook the remainder.

Serve with ice cream and the maple syrup pecans.

Gingerbread Pancakes

Ground ginger and molasses are the key to any gingerbread recipe. Grated fresh ginger or chopped stem ginger can be used to add a little texture.

285 g plain flour

2 teaspoons baking powder

½ teaspoon bicarbonate of soda

½ teaspoon salt

2 teaspoons ground ginger

2 teaspoons ground cinnamon

1 teaspoon ground cloves

2 eggs

55 g light brown sugar

250 ml buttermilk

2 tablespoons molasses
and cooled

To serve

warm apple marmalade (page 62)

cool crème fraîche

*a flat griddle pan or frying pan,
preheated and lightly greased*

Serves 4
Makes 12 pancakes

Sift the flour, baking powder, bicarbonate of soda, salt, ginger, cinnamon and cloves into a bowl. Put the eggs and brown sugar into a second bowl and whisk well with a wire whisk. Whisk in the buttermilk, molasses, cooled melted butter and 125 ml water. Add the flour mixture and whisk once or twice until almost smooth. Do not overwork the mixture – remember lumps are good.

Heat the prepared griddle or frying pan over medium heat. Reduce the heat. Pour about 2 tablespoons of batter into the pan, spread with the back of a spoon and cook in batches of 3–4 for 1 minute over low heat, until small bubbles begin to appear on the surface and the underside is golden brown. Turn them over and cook the other side for 1 minute. Transfer to a plate and keep them warm in a low oven while you cook the remainder.

Serve with apple marmalade and crème fraîche.

Triple Chocolate Pancakes

Complete chocolate overload! Packed with velvety melted chocolate and finished with sweet and sour taste of smooth white chocolate yoghurt. Adults only.

285 g plain flour

75 g cocoa powder

1 teaspoon
baking powder

1 teaspoon
bicarbonate of soda

55 g caster sugar

200 ml milk

125 ml buttermilk

2 eggs, separated

30 g unsalted butter,
melted and cooled

½ teaspoon salt

100 g dark chocolate,
chopped

100 g white
chocolate, chopped

hot chocolate sauce
(page 60), to serve

White chocolate
yoghurt

150 g white chocolate

4 tablespoons Greek
yoghurt

*blini pans (12 cm
diameter), a flat
griddle pan or frying
pan, preheated and
lightly greased*

Serves 4–6

**Makes about 12
pancakes**

Sift the flour, cocoa, baking powder, bicarbonate of soda and sugar into a bowl. Put the milk, buttermilk, egg yolks and cooled melted butter into a second large bowl and beat well. Add the flour mixture and mix thoroughly.

Put the egg whites and salt into a clean bowl and whisk until stiff peaks form. Add 1 tablespoon of the egg whites to the chocolate mixture and stir to loosen it, then carefully fold in the remaining egg whites, then the dark and white chocolate.

Heat the prepared blini pans, griddle or frying pan over medium heat. Reduce the heat. Pour about 2 tablespoons of batter into the pan and cook in batches of 3–4 over low heat for about 1 minute, or until small bubbles begin to appear on the surface and the underside is golden brown. Turn the pancakes over and cook the other side for 1 minute. Transfer to a plate and keep them warm in a low oven while you cook the remainder.

To make white chocolate yoghurt, put the chocolate into a bowl set over a saucepan of simmering water and melt slowly. Remove from the heat and let cool a little, then beat in the yoghurt until smooth and shiny. Serve with the pancakes and hot chocolate sauce.

Silver Dollar Pancakes

Although these mini-pancakes are a children's favourite, many adults harbour a secret passion for them as well.

150 g plain flour

1½ teaspoons baking powder

2 tablespoons caster sugar

½ teaspoon salt

2 eggs, separated

172 ml milk

unsalted butter, for frying

blueberry sauce (page 62), to serve

Whipped butter (optional)

200 g unsalted butter, softened

2 tablespoons milk

a flat griddle pan or frying pan, preheated and lightly greased

Serves 4–6

Makes 40 small pancakes

Sift the flour, baking powder, sugar and salt into a bowl. Put the egg yolks and milk into another bowl and gently beat in the sifted dry ingredients. Put the egg whites into a clean bowl and whisk with a wire whisk until stiff peaks form. Fold them into the batter with a metal spoon.

Heat the prepared griddle or frying pan over medium heat. Reduce the heat. Pour 1 teaspoon of batter into the pan and cook in batches of 6–8 for 2 minutes over low heat, until small bubbles begin to appear on the surface and the underside is golden brown. Turn the pancakes over and cook the other side for 1 minute. Transfer to a plate and keep them warm in a low oven while you cook the remainder, brushing the pan with butter as necessary.

Meanwhile, to make the whipped butter, put the butter and milk into a small bowl and whisk until pale and light.

Serve the pancakes with whipped butter and blueberry sauce or your choice of other accompaniments.

These pretty speckled pancakes are a treat. Orange zest gives the recipe a fresh edge while the poppy seeds provide a little crunch. Beware of the honey – too much and the pancakes will brown too quickly without giving the centre enough time to cook.

Poppyseed Pancakes
with Spiced Clementines

150 g plain flour

½ teaspoon baking powder

½ teaspoon bicarbonate of soda

30 g soft brown sugar

50 g poppyseeds

1 egg

1 tablespoon honey

80 ml sour cream

80 ml milk

250 g mascarpone cheese, to serve

Spiced clementines

4 clementines or small oranges

4 tablespoons spiced brown sugar (page 61)

a flat griddle or frying pan, preheated and lightly greased

Serves 4
Makes 10–12 small pancakes

To make the spiced clementines, grate the zest of 2 of the fruit for use in the pancakes, then peel all 4, removing as much of the bitter white pith as possible. Using a sharp knife, finely slice the fruit crossways. Arrange the fruit on a plate, sprinkle with the spiced sugar and set aside to infuse.

To make the pancakes, sift the flour, baking powder and bicarbonate of soda into a large bowl, then stir in the brown sugar and poppyseeds.

Put the egg, honey, sour cream and milk into a second large bowl, then add the reserved grated zest of the clementines. Whisk well, then add the flour mixture all at once and keep whisking until just smooth.

Heat the prepared griddle or frying pan over medium heat. Reduce the heat. Pour 1 tablespoon of batter into the pan and cook in batches of 3–4 for 1 minute over low heat, until small bubbles begin to appear on the surface and the underside is golden brown. Turn the pancakes over and cook the other side for 1 minute. Transfer to a plate and keep them warm in a low oven while you cook the remainder.

To serve, layer the poppyseed pancakes with slices of clementines and spoonfuls of mascarpone.

Overnight Pancakes

with Tropical Fruit and Mango and Ginger Purée

300 g plain flour

2 tablespoons caster sugar or vanilla sugar

1 teaspoon easy-blend dried yeast

1 teaspoon salt

375 ml milk

85 g unsalted butter, melted and cooled, plus extra for frying

2 eggs

To serve

assorted tropical fruit, such as mango, starfruit (carambola), kiwifruit, passionfruit and papaya

mango and ginger purée (page 63)

2 tablespoons sesame seeds, pan-toasted in a dry frying pan

a flat griddle pan or frying pan, preheated and lightly greased

Serves 4–6
Makes 10–12 pancakes

I love yeasted recipes because it means all the hard work is done the night before, so breakfast is a breeze. Mango and ginger purée takes seconds to prepare. I like to do this recipe when I have a house full of people – it's perfect for a summer morning.

Sift the flour, sugar, yeast and salt into a large bowl, then carefully mix in the milk and melted butter to make a thick batter. Cover the bowl and leave at room temperature overnight.

Next morning, separate the eggs and stir the yolks into the batter. Put the egg whites into a clean bowl, whisk with a wire whisk until stiff peaks form, then gently fold them in with a metal spoon.

Heat the prepared griddle or frying pan over medium heat. Reduce the heat. Pour about 2–3 tablespoons of batter into the pan and cook in batches of 3–4 for 1 minute over low heat, until small bubbles begin to appear on the surface and the underside is golden brown. Turn the pancakes over and cook the other side for about 2 minutes. Transfer to a plate and keep them warm in a low oven while you cook the remainder.

Serve immediately with fresh fruit and a spoonful of mango and ginger purée, sprinkled with pan-toasted sesame seeds.

150 g plain flour

65 g ground rice or semolina

40 g light muscovado sugar

$\frac{1}{2}$ teaspoon freshly grated nutmeg

1 tablespoon baking powder

$\frac{1}{2}$ teaspoon salt

1 egg

125 ml milk

125 ml plain yoghurt

4 small ripe bananas,
2 mashed, 2 sliced

unsalted butter, for frying

Toffee walnut sauce

15 g unsalted butter

85 g walnuts, coarsely chopped

1 recipe toffee sauce (page 61)

*a flat griddle pan or frying pan,
preheated and lightly greased*

Serves 4

Makes 8 small or 4 large pancakes

Sift the flour, ground rice, sugar, nutmeg, baking powder and salt into a large bowl. Put the egg, milk and yoghurt into another bowl, beat well, then add the 2 mashed bananas. Beat the flour mixture into the egg mixture – don't be tempted to beat it smooth!

Heat the prepared griddle or frying pan over medium heat. Reduce the heat. Pour 2 tablespoons of batter into the pan and press 3 slices of banana onto the pancake. Cook in batches of 3–4 for about 1 minute over low heat, or until small bubbles begin to appear on the surface and the underside is golden brown. Turn the pancakes over and cook the other side for about 2–3 minutes. They are about 10 cm diameter – cook as many as your pan will hold at once and transfer to a plate and keep them warm in a low oven while you cook the remainder. To make large pancakes, use 4 tablespoons each.

Meanwhile, to make the toffee walnut sauce, melt the butter in a large frying pan, add the nuts and stir over high heat until they smell toasted and are lightly browned. Drain the nuts on kitchen paper. Warm the toffee sauce in a saucepan over low heat and stir in the nuts.

Serve the pancakes, banana side up, with toffee walnut sauce.

Banana Pancakes
with Toffee Walnut Sauce

Whenever Americans find themselves in the
wilder parts of the world and they start to pine
for familiar food, it's apple pie and banana
pancakes that remind them of home. These
are a dressed-up version, glamorous enough
for a special brunch party – or just for a
weekend breakfast for the family.

Add sliced fruit to the top of any pancake to turn it into something special. Some fruits burn more quickly than others, so take care.

Date and Pistachio Griddle Cakes

200 g plain flour

2 teaspoons baking powder

1 teaspoon salt

3 tablespoons light brown sugar

50 g rolled oats

100 g shelled, unsalted pistachio nuts, coarsely chopped

100 g pitted dates, finely chopped

250 ml milk

2 eggs

55 g unsalted butter, melted and cooled, plus extra for brushing

grated zest of 1 lemon

2 apples

To serve

fresh honeycomb (optional)

Greek yoghurt or sour cream

a star-shaped biscuit cutter

a flat griddle pan or frying pan, preheated and lightly greased

Serves 4

Makes 12 griddle cakes

Sift the flour, baking powder and salt into a large bowl, then stir in the sugar, oats, nuts and dates. Put the milk, eggs, cooled melted butter and lemon zest into another bowl, beat well, then add the nut and oat mixture and stir gently. (Be careful not to overwork the mixture – it doesn't matter if the dough isn't smooth.)

Before you begin to cook the griddle cakes, prepare the apple by slicing it horizontally into 3 mm rings and removing the core of each slice with a pastry cutter (a star shape works best).

Heat the prepared griddle or frying pan over medium heat. Reduce the heat. Pour 1 tablespoon of batter onto the griddle and top with an apple slice. Cook in batches of 3–4 for 2–3 minutes over low heat, or until small bubbles begin to appear on the surface and the underside is golden brown. Brush the apple slice with a little melted butter, then turn the pancakes over and cook the other side for about 2 minutes. Repeat until all the mixture and apple slices have been used. Transfer to a plate and keep them warm in a low oven while you cook the remainder.

Serve immediately with honeycomb, if using, and Greek yoghurt.

200 g pine nuts

75 g plain flour

2 teaspoons baking powder

½ teaspoon salt

100 g instant polenta

2 tablespoons caster sugar

100 ml milk

2 eggs

30 g unsalted butter, melted and cooled

grated zest of 1 orange

To serve

icing sugar

orange and cardamom syrup (page 62)

a flat griddle pan or large frying pan, preheated and lightly greased

Makes 40 pancakes

Put the pine nuts into a dry frying pan and cook over a low heat, stirring constantly, until just brown. Transfer to a plate and let cool.

Sift the flour, baking powder and salt into a bowl and stir in the polenta and sugar.

Put the milk, eggs, cooled melted butter and orange zest into a bowl, beat well, then add the polenta mixture and beat until smooth. Stir in 150 g of the pine nuts and let the mixture stand for 5 minutes to soften the polenta and thicken the batter.

Heat the prepared griddle or frying pan over medium heat. Reduce the heat. Pour 1 tablespoon of batter onto the pan and sprinkle with a few of the remaining pine nuts. Cook in batches of 6–8 for about 2 minutes over low heat, or until small bubbles begin to appear on the surface and the underside is golden brown. Turn the pancakes over and cook the other side for about 2 minutes. Transfer to a plate and keep them warm in a low oven while you cook the remainder.

Serve sprinkled with sifted icing sugar, with the syrup poured over or served separately.

Pine Nut and Polenta Pennycakes

Bite-sized, nutty pancakes dredged in icing sugar are perfect to finish off a supper with friends. Serve the pennycakes with a huge bowl of cardamom syrup for communal dipping.

Cornmeal and Bacon Breakfast Stack

Masa harina and chilli give this recipe a slightly Mexican flavour. Try these pancakes with huevos rancheros or even avocado salsa.

100 g plain flour

1½ teaspoons baking powder

1 teaspoon salt

60 g masa harina or fine yellow cornmeal

1 egg, separated

100 ml buttermilk

200 ml milk

2 tablespoons freshly grated Parmesan cheese

150 g pancetta or streaky bacon, coarsely chopped

4 spring onions, cut into 1 cm slices

1 medium green chilli, deseeded and finely sliced

To serve

4 large portobello mushrooms

250 g cherry tomatoes on the vine

a few sage leaves, torn

4 eggs

olive oil, for frying and roasting

sea salt and freshly ground black pepper

a flat griddle pan or large frying pan, preheated and lightly greased

4 oiled muffin rings, 9 cm diameter

Serves 4

Makes 4 pancakes

Sift the flour, baking powder and salt into a large bowl, then stir in the masa harina or cornmeal. Put the egg yolks into another bowl, add the buttermilk and milk and beat well. Add the flour mixture and beat to a thick batter. Stir in the Parmesan. Put the egg white into a clean bowl and whisk until stiff peaks form, then fold into the batter using a metal spoon.

Meanwhile arrange the mushrooms in a roasting tin, stem side up. Sprinkle with olive oil, salt and pepper and roast in a preheated oven at 200°C (400°F) Gas 6 for 5 minutes. Add the tomatoes to the roasting tin, brush with a little extra olive oil, sprinkle with salt, pepper and the torn sage leaves, then roast for a further 5 minutes.

Heat the prepared griddle or frying pan over medium heat. Add the oiled muffin rings and heat well. Divide the bacon between the 4 muffin rings and fry for 1 minute. Add a share of the spring onions and chilli, then add 2 tablespoons of the batter to each ring. When the mixture has risen and started to set, remove the rings. Turn the pancakes over and cook until brown. Transfer to a plate and keep them warm in a low oven while you cook the eggs.

Meanwhile, brush a large frying pan with oil and heat well over high heat, then add the eggs and fry until the whites are set and the yolks still soft.

Put 1 pancake onto each plate. Add a mushroom, then put an egg on top. Finish the stack with a bunch of roasted tomatoes, then serve.

Belgian waffles are traditionally made in a deep, square waffle iron, which produces a thick waffle with deep wells to trap butter and syrup. The best use a yeast-raised batter, but don't let that put you off – it's definitely worth the effort. By doing the hard work the night before, all you need to do in the morning is add the eggs and bake.

Classic Belgian Waffles
with Strawberries and Praline Cream

Start the night before. Sift the flour, sugar, salt and yeast into a large bowl. Stir in the cooled melted butter, milk and vanilla extract to make a smooth mixture. Cover the bowl with clingfilm and leave at room temperature overnight.

First thing in the morning, turn on the lightly greased waffle iron. Beat the egg yolks into the yeast mixture. Put the egg whites into a clean bowl and whisk until stiff peaks form. Carefully fold them into the batter with a metal spoon.

To make the praline cream, put the cream into a clean bowl and whip to a soft, loose consistency. Add the praline and stir it once or twice to give a marbled effect, then set aside and let the caramel bleed into the cream.

Before baking the waffles, assemble all the toppings and accompaniments – the best waffles are eaten the moment they're done.

Depending on the size of the waffle iron, pour about 125 ml of batter into each heated compartment, close the lid (which will help spread out the batter) and cook until golden, about 3–5 minutes. Resist the temptation to open the lid for 3 minutes. There is nothing worse than an undercooked waffle: they should be crisp on the outside and served immediately. At a pinch, they can be kept warm in a low oven, but will lose some crispness. A quick reheating in the toaster works remarkably well.

Serve the waffles hot with a spoonful of praline cream and a few fresh strawberries.

285 plain flour

2 tablespoons caster sugar

1 teaspoon salt

1 teaspoon easy-blend dried yeast

140 g unsalted butter, melted and cooled

375 ml milk

1 teaspoon vanilla extract

3 eggs, separated

250 g strawberries, to serve

Praline Cream

300 ml double cream

55 g hazelnut praline (page 62)

a deep Belgian waffle iron, preheated and lightly greased

Serves 4–6
Makes 12 waffles

wonderful waffles

Crisp Chocolate Waffles

As we all know, when it comes to chocolate, some people become quite irrational – chocolate is their passion. This recipe is for them. Always use the best quality chocolate you can find – remember the higher the cocoa solid content, the better the chocolate.

285 g plain flour

2 tablespoons caster sugar

25 g cocoa powder

1 teaspoon salt

1 sachet (7 g) easy-blend dried yeast

85 g unsalted butter

150 g dark chocolate, chopped

375 ml cups milk

1 teaspoon vanilla extract

3 eggs, separated

To serve

hot chocolate sauce (page 60)

ice cream

a waffle iron, preheated and lightly greased

Serves 4

Makes 8–10 waffles

Start the night before. Sift the flour, sugar, cocoa powder, salt and yeast into a large bowl. Put the butter and 50 g of the chocolate into a large saucepan and melt over gentle heat. Stir in the milk and vanilla extract. Beat the flour mixture into the warm chocolate, then transfer to a large bowl and cover with clingfilm. Set aside at room temperature overnight.

First thing in the morning, turn on the lightly greased waffle iron. Beat the egg yolks into the yeast mixture and stir in the remaining chopped chocolate. Put the egg whites into a clean bowl and whisk with a wire whisk until stiff peaks form. Gently fold them into the batter with a metal spoon.

Depending on the size of the waffle iron, pour about 125 ml of the batter into each heated compartment, close the lid (which will help spread out the batter) and cook until crisp, about 4 minutes.

Serve the waffles cut or torn in half to reveal oozing melted chocolate. Add ice cream and smother with hot chocolate sauce.

You will probably find you have all the ingredients for a basic waffle mix in your kitchen already, So this is truly a speedy recipe. I find that a light oil spray is best for greasing the waffle iron.

Quick Vanilla Waffles

with Chilli-steeped Raspberries

285 g plain flour

2 teaspoons baking powder

½ teaspoon salt

1 tablespoon caster sugar

3 eggs, separated

225 ml milk

55 g unsalted butter, melted and cooled

2 teaspoons pure vanilla extract

To serve

icing sugar, for dusting

vanilla ice cream

chilli-steeped raspberries (page 63)

a waffle iron, preheated and lightly greased

Serves 6–8

Makes 24 heart-shaped sandwiches

Sift the flour, baking powder, salt and caster sugar into a large bowl. Put the egg yolks, milk, cooled melted butter and vanilla extract into another bowl and mix well. Add the flour mixture to the milk mixture and beat until just mixed – don't overbeat.

Put the egg whites into a clean bowl and whisk until stiff peaks form. Gently fold the egg whites into the waffle batter with a wooden spoon. It's important not to overmix at this stage, so if there are a few lumps of egg white floating around, leave them – it doesn't matter.

Spoon the batter into the preheated waffle iron, spread the mixture out to the edges and close the lid. (Most waffle irons take about 125 ml batter.) Electric waffle irons usually have an indicator light which goes off when the waffle is ready: if not, cook until the waffle is crisp and golden, about 3–5 minutes.

Sift the icing sugar over the waffles, top with ice cream and raspberries and serve. Alternatively, if you have a heart-shaped waffle, break it into segments and sandwich the hearts together with ice cream. Top with the raspberries.

Spicy Nut Waffles with Ginger Pears

Not all yeast batters need to be left for hours – you can cheat and still get some great results. The secret is to make sure everything is warm before you start, right down to the flour and the bowl – use the microwave defrost setting to raise the mixture in half the time.

Put the flour into a large microwavable bowl and warm on 100 per cent setting for 10 seconds: this will help the yeast grow and speed the rising process.

Put the warm milk, vanilla, cooled melted butter and egg yolks into another bowl and mix well. Add the yeast, salt, sugar, cinnamon and walnuts to the warm flour. Transfer the flour mixture to the milk mixture and stir until smooth. Cover with clingfilm and leave in a warm place for 45 minutes until doubled in size.

Put the wine into a saucepan large enough to fit the pears. Add 300 ml water, the sugar and ginger and bring slowly to the boil over medium heat. Peel the pears and add them to the pan. Reduce the heat and simmer for 25 minutes, gently turning the pears from time to time, to make sure they cook evenly. Using a slotted spoon, carefully remove the pears to a plate. Boil the ginger liquid for 10 minutes to reduce it to a thin syrup. Strain to remove the ginger, then return the pears and syrup to the pan and let steep until ready to serve.

To finish the mixture, put the egg whites into a clean bowl and whisk with a wire whisk until stiff peaks form. Fold through the batter with a metal spoon.

Depending on the size of the waffle iron, spoon about 125 ml of the mixture into the preheated compartments and cook until golden, about 4–5 minutes. Serve each waffle soaked in ginger syrup, topped with a pear or pears, a share of the crystallized or glacé ginger, and topped with a large spoonful of yoghurt or whipped cream.

285 g plain flour

310 ml warm milk

1 teaspoon vanilla extract

100 g unsalted butter, melted and cooled

2 eggs, separated

1 teaspoon easy-blend dried yeast

½ teaspoon salt

2 tablespoons caster sugar

2 teaspoons ground cinnamon

200 g walnuts, finely chopped

Ginger pears

½ bottle sweet wine (375 ml), such as orange muscat

3 mini pears or 1 large pear per person

120 g sugar

6 cm piece of fresh ginger, peeled and finely sliced

To serve

150 g crystallized or glacé ginger, finely sliced

yoghurt or whipped cream

a waffle iron, preheated and lightly greased

Serves 4–6

Makes 6–8 waffles

This recipe makes a delicate waffle, jam-packed with fruit. As the batter cooks, the raspberries soften and the juice seeps into the fabric of the waffle giving a beautiful mottled effect.

Raspberry Waffles
with Pistachio and Peach Honey

285 g plain flour

2 teaspoons baking powder

½ teaspoon salt

3 tablespoons caster sugar

3 eggs, separated

225 ml milk

55 g unsalted butter, melted and cooled

2 teaspoons vanilla extract

150 g fresh raspberries

To serve

crème fraîche

peach and pistachio honey (page 63)

a waffle iron, preheated and lightly greased

Serves 4
Makes 8 waffles

Sift the flour, baking powder, salt and sugar into a large bowl. Put the egg yolks, milk, cooled melted butter and vanilla extract into another bowl and beat well, then stir in the dry ingredients until almost mixed.

Add the raspberries to the mixture, crushing some with a spoon to give a marbled effect.

Put the egg whites into a clean bowl and whisk with a wire whisk until stiff peaks form. Gently fold into the batter with a large metal spoon.

Depending on the size of the waffle iron, spoon about 4–8 tablespoons of the batter into the preheated compartments and cook until crisp, about 4–5 minutes.

Serve with crème fraîche and peach and pistachio honey.

Spiced Pumpkin Waffles

285 g plain flour

3 teaspoons baking powder

½ teaspoon bicarbonate of soda

1 teaspoon ground cinnamon

1 teaspoon freshly grated nutmeg

1 teaspoon ground ginger

a pinch of salt

½ teaspoon freshly ground black pepper

2 eggs

55 g light muscovado sugar

250 g roasted pumpkin flesh, fresh or canned (see recipe introduction)

375 ml milk

55 g unsalted butter, melted and cooled

freshly grated zest of 1 orange

50 g pumpkin seeds (optional)

To serve

honey butter (page 60)

whipped cream (optional)

a waffle iron, preheated and lightly greased

Serves 3–4
Makes 6–8 waffles

I first discovered these on Hallowe'en in San Francisco a few years ago. They are packed with spices and I think are best served simply with cool whipped cream and sugar. If the thought of attacking a pumpkin and cooking it fills you with apathy, you can use canned or, better still, use raw grated butternut squash or pumpkin. If you do, put it into a clean cloth and squeeze out the excess liquid (so the waffles won't be limp).

Sift the flour, baking powder, bicarbonate of soda, cinnamon, nutmeg, ginger, salt and pepper into a large bowl. Put the eggs, sugar, pumpkin, milk, cooled melted butter and orange zest into another bowl and whisk well with a wire whisk. Gently fold in the flour mixture with a metal spoon.

Depending on the size of the waffle iron, spoon about 4–8 tablespoons of the batter into the preheated compartments and sprinkle with a few pumpkin seeds, if using. Cook until crisp, about 4–5 minutes. To achieve a frilly effect at the edges, as shown, use a little less mixture in the waffle iron.

Smother in honey butter, and serve with whipped cream, if using.

I love my pizzelle machine. It makes crisp wafers that can be moulded into cones for ice cream. They also make quick cannoli shells. Cannoli are a favourite Italian treat enjoyed all over the world, consisting of fried pastry tubes stuffed with sweet ricotta and chocolate chips. Making the shells is beyond most home cooks, but, while not traditional, these 'faux' cannoli are delicious and very pretty.

2 eggs

100 g caster sugar

65 g unsalted butter, cooled

1 teaspoon finely grated orange zest

1 teaspoon vanilla extract

300 g plain flour

½ teaspoon ground cinnamon

1 teaspoon baking powder

Cannoli filling

500 g ricotta cheese

300 ml double cream

50 g icing sugar, sifted

1 teaspoon almond essence

1 teaspoon ground cinnamon

200 g dark chocolate, grated

100 g shelled, unsalted pistachio nuts, finely chopped

an electric pizzelle maker, preheated and lightly greased

a piping bag fitted with a large plain nozzle

Makes 20

Pizzelle Cannoli

Put the eggs and sugar into a bowl and, using an electric whisk, beat until pale. Add the cooled butter, orange zest and vanilla. Sift in the flour, cinnamon and baking powder, then, using a wooden spoon, beat well to form a dough.

Flour your hands, then pinch off small, walnut-sized balls of dough. Squash each ball between your palms to form a disc. Put 1 disc in each heated compartment of the machine, then press the lid down and clip closed to spread the mixture into wafer-like biscuits. Cook for 1–3 minutes, depending on the machine.

Remove the hot wafers and immediately wrap each one around a clean saucepan handle or the handle of a wooden spoon to make an open-ended tube. (As the wafer cools it will become brittle, so it is important to act swiftly.) Let cool completely, then use immediately or store in an airtight container for up to 1 month.

To make the filling, use the back of a wooden spoon to push the ricotta through a sieve into a bowl. Add the cream, icing sugar, almond essence and cinnamon, and beat until thick and creamy. (The mixture will remain fairly grainy so don't be alarmed.) Stir in half the grated chocolate and transfer the filling to a piping bag fitted with a large plain nozzle. Pipe the filling into both ends of the cannoli and make sure the whole tube is filled. Dip the ends in chopped pistachios or the remaining grated chocolate, then serve.

Buttermilk Waffles with Baked Amaretti Apricots

Buttermilk gives a wonderful tangy richness to this waffle, while cornmeal provides extra bite. Fabulous served sweet or savoury. (Don't be tempted to undercook them – they benefit from a little extra time in the waffle iron.)

210 g plain flour

2 teaspoons baking powder

1 teaspoon bicarbonate of soda

½ teaspoon salt

2 tablespoons vanilla sugar (page 61) or sugar

75 g instant polenta or coarse cornmeal

375 ml buttermilk

30 g butter, melted and cooled

3 eggs, separated

Baked amaretti apricots

6 large apricots, halved

125 g blackberries or blueberries

250 g mascarpone cheese

4 amaretti biscuits, crushed

4 tablespoons pure maple syrup

To serve

icing sugar, sifted

maple syrup

a baking sheet

a waffle iron, lightly greased and preheated

Serves 4–8
Makes 8 large waffles

To prepare the apricots, put them onto a baking sheet, cut side up. Put the blackberries, mascarpone, crushed amaretti biscuits and maple syrup into a bowl and mix well. Spoon the mixture onto the apricots and bake in a preheated oven at 220°C (425°F) Gas 7 for about 10 minutes.

To make the waffles, sift the flour, baking powder, bicarbonate of soda, salt and sugar into a large bowl and stir in the polenta. Put the buttermilk, cooled melted butter and egg yolks into another bowl and beat well. Stir the flour mixture into the buttermilk mixture, then beat to form a smooth batter.

Put the egg whites into a clean bowl and whisk with a wire whisk until stiff peaks form. Gently fold the egg whites into the waffle batter with a metal spoon, being careful not to overmix.

Depending on the size of the waffle iron, spoon 4–8 tablespoons of the batter into the preheated compartments, so it almost covers the base. Cook until golden, about 3–4 minutes.

Pile the waffles onto heated plates, add the baked apricots and sprinkle with icing sugar. Serve with extra maple syrup on the side.

To make the sugar plums, put the quartered plums and spiced brown sugar into a bowl and toss to coat. Melt the butter in a small frying pan over medium heat until it foams, then add all the plum pieces and gently sauté until caramelized. Add the lemon juice to loosen the butter syrup and set aside to keep warm while you prepare the waffles.

To make the waffles, put the plain and wholemeal flours into a large bowl, add the baking powder, salt, sugar, allspice and pecan nuts and stir well.

Put the egg yolks into another bowl, add the milk, molasses and cooled melted butter and beat well. Add the flour mixture, stir well, then stir in the chopped apple. Put the egg whites into a clean bowl and whisk with a wire whisk until stiff peaks form, then fold gently into the waffle batter with a metal spoon.

Depending on the size of the waffle iron, spoon about 125 ml of the batter into the preheated compartments, making sure each batch has lots of apple in it. Cook until crisp, about 3–5 minutes.

Serve the waffles immediately, topped with warm plums and plenty of sticky plum juice.

225 g plain flour

75 g wholemeal flour

2 teaspoons baking powder

½ teaspoon salt

2 tablespoons soft dark brown sugar

1 teaspoon ground allspice

50 g pecan nuts, chopped

2 eggs, separated

200 ml milk

1 tablespoon molasses

55 g unsalted butter, melted and cooled

2 crisp apples, peeled, cored and coarsely chopped

Sugar Plums

6 ripe plums, quartered and pitted

110 g spiced brown sugar (page 61)

30 g unsalted butter

freshly squeezed juice of ½ lemon

a waffle iron, lightly greased and preheated

Serves 4–6

Makes 8 waffles (deep Belgian size)

Apple Wholemeal Waffles with Sugar Plums

I always associate this recipe with autumn, when all kinds of orchard fruits are in season. Allspice is the secret ingredient – it brings all the fruit and nut flavours together, and grinding your own allspice berries will make sure you get the full force of the spice. I keep a special pepper grinder just for allspice.

Grilling bacon in a waffle iron is no new thing, in fact it's very logical when you think about it. Not only does it allow the smokiness of the pancetta to penetrate the waffle, but saves on washing up frying pans too! Use thinly sliced pancetta to ensure it cooks through.

Smoked Pancetta Waffles

with Blackberry Maple Pour

255 g plain flour

2 teaspoons baking powder

1 teaspoon bicarbonate of soda

1/2 teaspoon salt

1 tablespoon caster sugar

1/2 teaspoon English mustard powder

50 g Parmesan cheese, grated

55 g ground semolina

3 eggs, separated

225 ml buttermilk

4 tablespoons olive oil

16 slices finely sliced smoked pancetta or streaky bacon

maple and blackberry pour (page 62), to serve

a waffle iron, lightly greased and preheated

Serves 4
Makes 8 waffles

Sift the flour, baking powder, bicarbonate of soda, salt, sugar and mustard into a bowl, then stir in the grated Parmesan and semolina.

Put the egg yolks, buttermilk and olive oil into a second bowl and whisk well. Add the flour mixture and beat well.

Put the egg whites into a clean bowl and whisk with a wire whisk until stiff peaks form, then fold into the mixture with a metal spoon.

Depending on the size of the waffle iron, spoon about 3 tablespoons of the batter into each preheated compartment, so it almost covers the base. The batter should be quite thick, so spread it out with the back of a spoon, leaving enough room for it to spread and rise. Put 2 slices of the pancetta on top of the batter, then carefully close the lid. Cook until crisp, 4–5 minutes (the pancetta should be sizzling crisp around the edges).

Serve the waffles immediately with warm maple and blackberry pour.

Cheese on toast has always been a popular comfort food, so what better way
start your weekend than with an oozing cheese waffle on which to build your
favourite brunch. Most cheeses – from cottage cheese to Parmesan – will work,
but for me a good strong Cheddar can't be beaten, especially with a touch of
cayenne pepper or English mustard powder to spark up the flavour.

Morning-after Breakfast Waffles

180 g plain flour

120 g fine cornmeal

2 teaspoons baking powder

½ teaspoon salt

2 eggs, separated

225 ml milk

200 ml sour cream or yoghurt

120 g Cheddar cheese, grated

2 tablespoons scissor-snipped
fresh chives

To serve

4 bunches cherry tomatoes,
on the vine

16 slices bacon

8 eggs

sea salt and freshly ground
black pepper

olive oil, for frying and roasting

a baking sheet, greased

*a waffle iron, preheated and
lightly greased*

Serves 4
Makes 8 waffles

Put the vine tomatoes onto a greased baking sheet, sprinkle with
olive oil, season with salt and pepper and roast in a preheated
oven at 200°C (400°F) Gas 6 for 5 minutes or until their skins blister.

To make the waffles, sift the flour, cornmeal, baking powder and
salt into a large bowl. Put the egg yolks into another bowl, add the
milk, sour cream and 2 tablespoons olive oil and whisk well. Add
the flour mixture and beat well. Put the egg whites into a clean
bowl and whisk with a wire whisk until stiff peaks form. Using a
large metal spoon, gently fold the egg whites, cheese and chives
into the waffle batter.

Brush a small frying pan with olive oil and heat well, add the bacon
and fry until crisp. Remove from the pan and let drain on kitchen
paper. Brush the pan with oil again, add 4 slices of the cooked
bacon, then break 2 eggs on top and fry gently until cooked. Set
aside to keep warm.

Depending on the size of the waffle iron, spoon about 125 ml of the
batter into the preheated compartments. Cook until crisp, at least
4–5 minutes (cheese waffles taste so much better when well done).
Transfer to a large plate, slide the bacon and eggs on top and serve
with the roasted tomatoes. Repeat to make the other servings.

Crêpes Suzette

This old favourite seems to have disappeared in recent years, but it's still up there with the greats.

To make the basic crêpes, put the flour into a food processor, add the salt, egg, egg yolk, milk and water mixture and cooled melted butter and pulse for a few seconds until the batter is smooth. Chill for 30 minutes.

Heat the pan over medium heat, then lightly brush with butter, using kitchen paper to wipe away any excess. Spoon 2 tablespoons of the batter into the hot pan and quickly swirl it around to coat the base of the pan evenly but thinly. If you add too much batter just tip the extra back into the bowl and trim away the pouring trail. Cook the crêpe for 1 minute, then carefully turn it over and cook the other side. (Serve immediately with sugar and lemon, jam or chocolate, or use to make Crêpes Suzette or the Galette on the following page.)

To make the crêpe suzette sauce, put the butter, sugar, orange zest and juice and Curaçao into a large frying pan and gently warm through over low heat. When the sugar has dissolved, boil the mixture for 2 minutes to make a butter syrup.

Put the first crêpe into the pan of hot orange butter and, using a palette knife and fork, fold it into quarters and push it to the edge of the pan to make room for the next one. Repeat until all the crêpes are coated in orange butter and folded in the pan.

To finish, keep the pan over a low flame and sprinkle the crêpes with the sugar, Curaçao and rum. Quickly but very carefully, light the alcohol in the pan with a match. Serve immediately before the flames disappear.

110 g plain flour

½ teaspoon salt

1 egg

1 egg yolk

150 ml milk mixed with 150 ml water

30 g unsalted butter, melted and cooled

Crêpes suzette sauce

110 g unsalted butter

60 g caster sugar

grated zest and juice of 2 oranges

3 tablespoons Curaçao, other citrus liqueur, or apricot brandy

To finish

1 tablespoon caster sugar

2 tablespoons Curaçao, other citrus liqueur, or apricot brandy

1 tablespoon dark rum

a crêpe pan, omelette pan or small frying pan, preheated to moderately hot, buttered

Serves 4
Makes 8–10 crêpes

Note To store crêpes, just stack them on a large plate until you need to reheat them. They can be kept warm by wrapping them in a tea towel and putting them on a plate set over a saucepan of simmering water.

To freeze, stack with sheets of greaseproof paper between, wrap in clingfilm, then freeze.

crêpes, crumpets and blini

225 g plain flour

½ teaspoon salt

55 g caster sugar

4 eggs

550 ml milk

55 g unsalted butter, melted and cooled

2 tablespoons brandy

peanut oil, for brushing

Chocolate filling

4 egg yolks

110 g caster sugar

2 teaspoons vanilla extract

300 ml double cream

225 g dark chocolate, grated

200 g walnuts, finely chopped

To serve (optional)

250 ml double cream, lightly whipped

1 teaspoon ground cinnamon

finely grated zest of 1 orange

a crêpe pan or small frying pan, 20 cm diameter

a springform cake tin, 20 cm diameter, buttered and lined

buttered greaseproof paper

Serves 8

Chocolate Galette

This is literally a pancake-cake, layered with sweet custard and chocolate and baked in the oven. A wedge of this curious striped chocolate pudding makes a great talking point.

To make the batter, put the flour into a food processor, add the salt, sugar, eggs, milk, cooled melted butter and brandy and pulse for a few seconds until smooth. Heat the crêpe pan, brush with peanut oil, then wipe away with excess with kitchen paper. Cook the crêpes as in the Basic Crêpe recipe on page 52. You should have at least 15, depending on how thin you make them.

To make the filling, put the egg yolks and sugar into a bowl and whisk until pale and thick. Beat in the vanilla and cream.

Put a crêpe in the base of the prepared cake tin, spread it with a little vanilla cream mixture and sprinkle with grated chocolate and chopped walnuts. Repeat the layers until you run out of crêpes or fill the tin. Finish with a crêpe and cover it with a piece of buttered greaseproof paper.

Bake in a preheated oven at 180°C (350°F) Gas 4 for 30 minutes. Remove from the oven and let cool slightly before unclipping the tin and transferring the galette to a serving plate.

Serve sliced into wedges, topped with lightly whipped cream flavoured with cinnamon and orange zest, if using.

Good English crumpets remind me of my childhood, and this homemade version is even more wonderful than the shop-bought kind. I like to use fresh yeast – available in small bakers or sometimes from in-supermarket bakeries – but in case you can't find it, use easy-blend dried yeast instead.

Tea and Crumpets

285 ml milk mixed with 285 ml water

15 g fresh yeast*

450 g plain flour

½ teaspoon bicarbonate of soda

1 teaspoon salt

To serve

unsalted butter

berry jam or honey

tea

2–3 crumpet rings or scone cutters

a flat griddle pan or frying pan, preheated and greased

Makes 12

*To use easy-blend dried yeast, mix one 7 g sachet with the flour

Warm the milk and water mixture in a small saucepan. If using fresh yeast, put it into a small bowl with a little of the warm liquid, stir well, then add the remaining milk and water. Sift the flour into a mixing bowl, then stir in the warm yeast mixture. (I find the easiest way to get a smooth batter is to use your hand.)

Cover the bowl with a clean cloth and leave in a warm place for 1 hour. Put the bicarbonate of soda and salt into a bowl, add 2 tablespoons water, mix well, then beat it into the mixture. Set aside for a further 45 minutes.

Put the greased crumpet rings on the prepared griddle pan and set over medium heat. When the rings are hot, spoon 2 tablespoons of the batter into each ring – just enough to cover the base. Let cook for about 4–5 minutes, until the underside is golden, then remove the rings and turn the crumpet over to brown the top.

To serve, toast the crumpets on both sides, smother them with butter and stack on a hot plate. Serve with extra butter and a dish of berry jam or honey. A cup of tea is the traditional accompaniment.

100 g plain flour

100 g buckwheat flour

½ teaspoon salt

½ teaspoon fast-action dried yeast

1 tablespoon caster sugar

300 ml warm milk

2 tablespoons double cream, lightly whipped

1 egg, separated

sour cream, to serve

Dill Pickled Salmon

300 g thick-cut smoked salmon

1 tablespoon chopped dill

1 small cucumber, about 15 cm, chopped

2 tablespoons grated raw beetroot

Dressing

freshly squeezed juice of 2 limes

2 teaspoon caster sugar

1 mild red chilli, deseeded and finely chopped

sea salt and freshly ground black pepper

1–4 blini pans or a frying pan, lightly greased

Serves 4

Makes 4

The blin (plural blini) is probably the most famous food ever to come out of Russia. They are cooked in a small iron frying pan, called a blini pan, like the one in the picture. However, you don't need a special pan – blini cooked in an ordinary large frying pan or on a flat griddle taste just as authentic, even if they do look a bit freeform.

Buckwheat Blini

Sift the flour and buckwheat flour into a large bowl, add the salt, yeast and sugar. Make a hollow in the centre and add the warm milk, cream and egg yolk. Gradually mix into a smooth batter, cover with clingfilm and set aside in a warm place for 1 hour.

Whisk the egg white until stiff peaks form and fold it through the risen batter with a metal spoon. Fold in the whipped cream. Heat the prepared blini pan(s) over medium heat and spoon in enough mixture to cover the base of the pan. If making in a frying pan, each blin should be about 10 cm diameter. Turn it over when bubbles rise to the surface and the base lightly browned.

To make the dill pickled salmon, cut the salmon into 5 mm pieces and put into a medium bowl. Add the dill, cucumber and beetroot. To make the dressing, put the lime juice, sugar and chilli into a separate bowl and whisk with a fork. Add the dressing to the salmon mixture, toss gently, then add salt and pepper to taste.

Serve the warm blini with sour cream and a spoonful of the dill pickled salmon. Smoked salmon, sour cream and caviar are another traditional topping.

sauces and toppings

Honey Butter

250 g unsalted butter, softened
grated zest of 1 lemon
6 tablespoons thick clover honey
Makes 300 g

Put the butter and lemon zest into a food processor and process until smooth. With the motor running, add the honey and blend until pale. Transfer to a lidded container and store for up to 2 weeks in the refrigerator (it will set as it chills).

Hot or Cold Chocolate Sauce

300 ml double cream
1 tablespoon brandy
250 g dark chocolate, broken
1 tablespoon golden syrup
30 g unsalted butter
Serves 4–6: Makes 500 ml

Put the cream and brandy into a saucepan and heat until almost boiling. Add the chocolate, golden syrup and butter and stir until the the chocolate has melted and the sauce is smooth. Serve hot or cold.

Cinnabutter

250 g unsalted butter, softened
2 tablespoons milk
85 g icing sugar
4 teaspoons ground cinnamon
1 teaspoon freshly grated nutmeg
Makes 300 g

Put all the ingredients into a small bowl and beat with an electric whisk until pale and creamy. Transfer to a lidded container and store in the refrigerator. Alternatively, spoon it onto a piece of clingfilm, roll it into a log and chill (cut a slice when you need it). Keeps for 2 weeks in the refrigerator.

Hazelnut Praline

110 g hazelnuts
110 g caster sugar
Makes 220 g

Lightly oil a baking sheet. Put the nuts and sugar into a saucepan over low heat until the sugar melts. As it begins to brown, stir briefly with a metal spoon and continue cooking until the sugar is a good caramel colour. Pour the mixture onto the oiled baking sheet and let cool.

Break up the cold praline with a rolling pin, put the pieces into a plastic bag, wrap it in a tea towel and tap with the pin to form a coarse powder. Store in an airtight container.

Vanilla Sugar

600 g caster sugar
6 vanilla pods
Makes 600 g

Put the sugar into a food processor. Split the vanilla pods lengthways leaving them attached at one end. Using a sharp knife, scrape the seeds out of the pods and into the sugar. Set aside the pods. Blend briefly to distribute the vanilla seeds, then pack the sugar and the spent pods into a large glass jar. The longer you leave it, the stronger the flavour. It lasts for months, so make a large batch.

Spiced Brown Sugar

400 g light muscovado sugar
200 g dark muscovado sugar
2 cinnamon sticks, broken,
plus 2 whole sticks, to store
1 teaspoon allspice berries
1 teaspoon whole cloves
finely grated zest of 1 lemon
Makes 600 g

Put both sugars into a food processor, add the broken cinnamon sticks, allspice, cloves and lemon zest and grind to a coarse powder. Sift through a wide meshed sieve and discard any large pieces of spice. Store the spiced sugar in an airtight container with 2 cinnamon sticks.

Toffee Sauce

85 g unsalted butter
60 g demerara sugar
100 g golden syrup
60 ml double cream
Makes 250 ml

Put all the ingredients into a saucepan and heat gently, stirring constantly, until the sugar has dissolved. Boil for 3 minutes, then serve immediately or let cool and store in an airtight container in the refrigerator for up to 1 week.

Orange and Cardamom Syrup

400 g sugar
400 ml orange juice, strained
8 cardamom pods, bruised
finely peeled zest of 1 orange
Makes 600 ml

Put all the ingredients into a saucepan and heat gently over low heat until the sugar has dissolved. Increase the heat and boil the syrup for 10 minutes. Cool and store in the refrigerator for up to 2 weeks. Leave the zest and pods in the syrup while you store it, but strain before using. (The syrup will thicken further as it cools.)

Maple and Blackberry Pour

125 g blackberries
250 ml maple syrup
a piece of lemon zest
Makes 350 ml

Put all the ingredients into a saucepan and gently heat over low heat until the syrup is almost boiling and the berries have begun to let out their juice. Let the syrup stand for 5 minutes to infuse and cool slightly, remove the lemon zest and serve.

Apple Marmalade

30 g unsalted butter
3 cooking apples, peeled, cored and sliced
grated zest of ½ lemon
100 g light brown sugar
Makes 250 g

Melt the butter in a large saucepan over low heat and add the apples, lemon zest and 2 tablespoons water. Cook the apples until soft and pulpy, then press them through a sieve into a bowl. Beat in the sugar, return the mixture to a clean pan and boil until you have a thick purée. Cool slightly and serve or store in the refrigerator for up to 2 weeks.

Blueberry Sauce

1 tablespoon arrowroot
3 tablespoon vanilla sugar (page 60) or caster sugar
300 g blueberries
freshly squeezed juice of 1 lemon
Makes 500 ml

Put the arrowroot and 1 tablespoon water into a bowl and stir to make a thin paste. Transfer to a saucepan, add the sugar, blueberries and 300 ml water and bring to the boil, stirring constantly. Simmer for 10 minutes, remove from the heat and stir in the lemon juice. Serve hot or store in the refrigerator for up to 1 week.

Chilli-steeped Raspberries

2 bird's eye chillies, deseeded

150 g raspberries

2 tablespoons framboise or brandy

200 g sugar

Makes 350 ml

Put the chillies, raspberries and framboise into a bowl.
Put the sugar into a saucepan, add 200 ml water and
heat gently over low heat until the sugar has dissolved,
then boil for 5 minutes until thickened and reduced.
Pour the hot syrup over the raspberries, stir once, then
cover and leave for at least 2 hours to develop the
flavours. Remove the chillies before serving.

Mango and Ginger Purée

**2 ripe mangoes,
peeled and chopped**

**3 cm fresh ginger,
peeled and grated**

**freshly squeezed juice
of 1 lime**

**2 tablespoons
icing sugar**

Makes 400 ml

Put the mango into a blender. Squeeze the grated
ginger to extract the juice. Add the juice to the mango
and discard the gratings. Blend well, add the lime juice,
sugar and a little water if necessary. Strain the sauce
and serve immediately, or store in the refrigerator for
up to 2 days.

Peach and Pistachio Honey

2 firm peaches, skinned and pitted

350 ml clear orange blossom honey

**1 tablespoon peach schnapps
(optional)**

**50 g shelled unsalted
pistachio nuts***

Makes 500 ml

**Pistachios from a Middle Eastern
shop will be very bright green.*

Cut the peach flesh into 3 mm
cubes. Put the honey and
schnapps, if using, into a
saucepan and heat until almost
boiling. Add the chopped
peaches and pistachios and let
cool slightly. Serve warm as
a spooning sauce.

index